Jesus The King

Booklet Edition

Discover the greatest path of all

"Enter through the narrow gate. For wide is the gate and broad is the path that leads to destruction, and there are many who enter through it. For small is the gate and narrow is the path that leads to life, and there are few who find it"

—Jesus, the Messiah

David O'Brien

Then came Jesus forth, wearing the crown of thorns, and the purple robe. And Pilate said unto them, "Behold the man!"

—John 19:5

Remember Jesus the Christ ("The Messiah-King," "the Anointed King"), risen from the dead, descendant of King David, according to my gospel...

—2Timothy 2:8

And when they could not find them, they dragged Jason and some of the brothers before the city authorities, shouting, "These men who have turned the world upside down have come here also, and Jason has received them, and they are all acting against the decrees of Caesar, saying that there is another king, Jesus."

—Acts 17:6-7

All For The Prize Publications
allfortheprizepublications@gmail.com

Full version of Jesus the Messiah-King, including the section, "First Steps," is available for free download at **www.actschristianity.com**

Lesson 1

What Did Jesus Do?

Luke, a doctor and follower of King Jesus, wrote the book of the Bible known today as, "The Gospel of Luke." With the help of the Holy Spirit, he called it a record, "of all that Jesus began to do and teach" (Acts 1:1). Jesus did works, and he taught. When you consider a special person, a teacher or prophet, you must consider both their words and their life. What did King Jesus do? What did he teach?

Let's consider Jesus' life for now. The first amazing thing about Jesus' life is that he *fulfilled prophecy*, prophecy previously given about him. This is not true of most prominent people, but it *characterizes* the Messiah[1], Jesus.

So, what is prophecy? It's a message, through people, that comes from God.[2] It's sometimes a prediction of the future, but not always. From near the beginning of the fall of mankind, God has communicated to humanity through prophets—special servants of his who he gifted to speak his words at times. It was through them that he wrote the Bible, over a period of over a thousand years. I will be quoting it throughout this book, starting with this:

...knowing this first of all, that no prophecy of Scripture comes from someone's own interpretation. For no prophecy was ever

---

[1] "Messiah" (from Hebrew) means **"the King/Priest Chosen and Empowered by God."** In Greek, the word is "Christos," where we get the term, "the Christ." The literal is, "the Anointed One"

[2] "God" (Hebrew: "EL") literally means, "the Powerful One." He's the One who created everything, who's all- knowing and all-powerful, pure love, completely right and good, and full of justice...we'll talk more about him

produced by the will of man, but men spoke from God as they were carried along by the Holy Spirit. (2Peter 1:20-21[3])

Predictions about Jesus, actually, first began in the Garden of Eden, before mankind was sent out of it. Let me stop and ask the question, "Why were they—the first man and woman—expelled from Paradise?" It was for more than eating an apple! This is what happened: they were given everything—a perfect habitat, perfect bodies without pain or death, lives of adventure, relationship with God unlike any created beings on Earth, and the commission from God to rule on Earth as His representatives. Humans were created as royalty, as ambassadors of God's kingdom,[4] on Earth. They were commissioned to *subdue*, not the peaceful, created paradise but an army of rebellious fallen spirits. And God Himself would come down and spend periods of time with them. There was no division between original mankind and God. Their spiritual and physical senses were totally alive.

An amazing truth about God is that he, "tests the righteous."[5] He doesn't only test evil people. He tests the righteous. The first man and woman, who did everything right, who had everything, were tested. God told them they could eat of any tree of the Garden except one. They were given so much in the beginning, but they would soon lose it.

Eventually satan,[6] or "the devil,"[7] who was supposed to be subdued and dominated by the newly appointed representatives of

---

[3] Format means, "2nd Peter, chapter 1, verses 20 to 21."

[4] The political structure of God's country is a monarchy, a kingdom, of which He is the King

[5] Psalm 11:5, Jeremiah 20:12

[6] The name "satan" means, "the enemy" and "the resister." He resists God's purposes and people

God, approached the man and woman. This crafty being is called "the serpent," as well as "the dragon."[8] It came in and LIED to the first people. Tragically, the first man and woman *listened to* and soon *believed* the enemy over God, and then they took the plunge…

The effect of this act can be seen in every aspect of life and society today.

How must have Adam and Eve felt, as they heard God approaching them in the Garden for a time of sharing and hanging out? They knew what they'd done was wrong and that the serpent had lied to them. They must have felt extremely dirty, unable to come into the light of God's face. The Bible says they hid themselves when he came near.

A "curse" simply means a judgment. God blesses and curses— he decrees good things for people and bad things. He is the Great Judge. And, in fact, someday he will judge all people, angels and evil spirits. During that dark day in the Garden of Eden, God had to pronounce a negative judgment on Adam and Eve, all their descendants, and even the physical creation.

Another amazing truth about God is that he's merciful. To those who have failed the tests in their life, his hand of mercy is open and extended. He's not spiteful, abusive, explosive, or vindictive.[9] God actually "delights in showing mercy."[10] So alongside the judgment that he gave, he also extended mercy.

---

[7] The "devil" literally means "through throwing." In other words, he's a coward and doesn't approach his targets directly. He attacks from a ways away and uses deception

[8] Revelation 20:2

[9] Those are actually characteristics of the enemy, who first uses deception to take people down and then attacks and accuses them for falling! God is the opposite

[10] Micah 7:18

When He pronounced judgment on the serpent also, he foretold of a way out of the pain and torment that was coming to humanity! He said to the devil:

I will put enmity between you and the woman, and between your offspring and her Offspring; he shall bruise your head, and you shall bruise his heel. (Genesis 3:15)

Consider this. After the fall, mankind lost its place of dominance. They're still like God in some ways but can't naturally know him, and can't represent him and subdue the rebel, satan or his army. But God spoke of a time when an Offspring of Eve would come. He would be bruised on his heel, while *bruising the serpent's head!* When King Jesus was crucified unjustly, he was bruising satan's head, he was crushing it under his foot. His heel was bruised in the process—and it was real pain, the worst of all. But he was removing satan's place of dominance over the human race, by removing humanity's guilt, for all who believe! ☺

For the Messiah also suffered once for sins, the righteous for the unrighteous, that he might bring us to God. (1Peter 3:18)

Virtually every detail of King Jesus' earthly life was documented beforehand, by ancient Hebrew prophets. He fulfilled the words of God, so that those in Israel with sincere hearts after God would recognize him when he came, by what he did. What did he do, in addition to proclaiming his Message??? In one word: *miracles.*

Jesus returned to Galilee in the power of the Spirit, and news about him spread through the whole countryside. He was teaching in their synagogues, and everyone praised him. He went to Nazareth, where he had been brought up, and on the Sabbath day he went into the synagogue, as was his custom. He stood up to read, and the scroll of the prophet Isaiah was handed to him. Unrolling it, he found the place where it is written: *"The Spirit of the Lord is on me, because he has anointed me[11] to proclaim good news to the poor. He has sent me to proclaim freedom for the prisoners and recovery of sight for the blind, to set the oppressed free, to proclaim the year of the Lord's favor."* Then he rolled up the scroll, gave it back to the attendant and sat down. The eyes of everyone in the synagogue were fastened on him. He began by saying to them, "Today this scripture is fulfilled in your hearing." (Luke 4:14-21)

With power from God, he healed sick people of every kind of disease and evil spirit oppression. Some specific cases: he instantly cured a boy of leprosy. He healed a woman who for twelve years had a tormenting, bleeding problem. He healed a hunchback woman who'd been deformed for 18 years. He *raised a boy from the dead*, whose mother was a widow and had no one to care for her. He stopped a deadly storm on the sea. He removed evil spirits from an insane man, who could not be held by chains!

God's representative, Jesus, also forgave a woman who'd been in prostitution. Forgiveness is in itself a miracle. He forgave a paralyzed man of something he'd done and then healed him so he walked. He freed the tongues of many mute people and opened the

---

[11] God chose & empowered Jesus. He is "the Anointed One," the Messiah, sent from the Father into the world

ears of many deaf. He dealt with leprosy and all kinds of diseases. Imagine them: heart disease, lung problems, stomach cancer, teeth issues, foot problems, mental issues, and on and on. He was a Doctor—the best of them. These and many more of what Jesus did are recorded in Mathew, Mark, Luke, and John of the Bible.[12] And John stated at the end of his book:

Now there are also many other things that Jesus did. Were every one of them to be written, I suppose that the world itself could not contain the books that would be written. (John 22:25)

The greatest act that Jesus did, though, was not an obviously great one. It actually looked like a weak one. It wasn't raising someone from the dead, or healing anyone directly. It was that he became a sacrifice, a substitution for mankind. This was his greatest purpose in coming. All the people he healed eventually died. But he came to do something eternal. He came to deal with the root cause of every single problem that's ever been on Earth, and from there, to set a multitude of people from every nation free. How did he do this??

Therefore, just as sin came into the world through one man, and death through sin, and so death spread to all men because all sinned...as one trespass led to condemnation for all men, so one act of righteousness leads to justification[13] and life for all men. For as by the one man's disobedience the many were

---

[12] The first four books of what's often called, "The New Testament"
[13] "Justification" means "making right" or "making righteous"

made sinners, so by the one man's obedience the many will be made righteous. (Romans 5:12, 18-19)

By obeying God's command to Jesus, to *selflessly* die for humanity, Jesus reversed the effect of Adam's *selfish* act. Just as real as the fact that all humans sin and all humans die, is the fact that Jesus' death can make you righteous and give you indestructible life. This is what God sent Jesus to do. He wants to *give* you righteousness.

When he hung on that execution instrument, the cross, all of God's judgment for all of each human's sins was poured out on him. Is it no wonder, at one point, in agony, Jesus had to cry out and ask his Father why?

About the ninth hour Jesus cried out with a loud voice, saying, "Eli, Eli, lema sabachthani?" that is, "My God, my God, why have you forsaken me? (Matthew 27:46)

We see from earlier writings of prophets that God answered this prayer of his. At that time, as Jesus hung naked and mutilated on the cross, fulfilling his destiny as the Lamb of God, the Father opened Jesus' eyes, and he saw the future. What do you think he saw? He saw, "his offspring,"[14] those who his great work would make righteous, those who would believe in him and be saved by him. He saw you! Then it says, "he was satisfied."

Someone had to pay for the sins. You could do it. But God *is love*,[15] and his love for *you* was so great he gave you a solution.

---

[14] Isaiah 53:10-11, Hebrews 12:2
[15] 1John 4:16

For God so loved the world, that he gave his only Son, that whoever believes in him should not perish ["die"] but have eternal life. For God did not send his Son into the world to condemn the world, but in order that the world might be saved through him...*Whoever* believes in the Son has eternal life; *whoever* does not obey the Son shall not see life, but the wrath of God remains on him. (John 3:16-17, 36)

What is "the wrath of God"? Wrath means *fierce anger* and related to God's just judgment. God is pure and holy, beyond what any of us can imagine. That purity is in 180-degree opposition to evil. There's no evil in God, and none will be allowed to remain in His universe. Evil and those who live in it are doomed to be completely removed. But at this time, though the ship is going down, God has offered lifeboats to *ALL* humanity. He poured his wrath out on His Son, King Jesus. We can now escape the judgment of "perishing" forever, through Jesus.

This Messiah, this King was different than any other. He didn't lift himself up; he came on a mission to die—for you and me. As he said about Himself,

The Son of Man[16] came not to be served but to serve, and to give his life as a ransom for many. (Mark 10:43)

When he died a brutal death penalty, which he did not deserve, he was taking the role of a lamb sacrifice, a substitute, *for fallen*

---

[16] This is one of the titles of Jesus, which he often used about himself. "Man" is the same word in the original language as, "Adam." Jesus came as a descendent of Adam, in order to save the human or "adamic" race

humanity. He is the slain lamb.[17] As such, he is "the satisfying sacrifice for our sins."[18] In other words, he took the judgment due to Adam, Eve, and all humanity that followed, so that God sees the sacrifice and is fully satisfied. JESUS PAID THE PRICE FOR ALL HUMAN EVIL. God can lift the ban on humanity and give us full forgiveness, reunion with him, and eternal life.

Three days after his death, after he paid the full penalty for all of humanity's sins, King Jesus rose again. He's alive; the Father raised him from the dead and lifted him to the highest throne, his rightful place at the Father's side. He has supreme authority in Heaven and on Earth, as God's appointed King. At this time, he is not fully exerting his authority on Earth, because now is the temporary time period in which all have the right to hear the message about Him, confess Him as Lord, and be saved.

Do you see him? Do you see his mercy, how he stepped out of heaven for you, to take your place in the death sentence? Do you see that God, according to his promises spoken through his prophets, raised him from the dead? If you believe this in your heart, it's because God has revealed it to you. He wants a relationship with you. He sent his Son for you to bring you back to him. His door is open WIDE to you. Enter in and know God. Receive the gift he has freely given.

We've all sinned in different ways. But one thing we all have in common is we've gone astray from God. So we ALL have to repent, to make a heart-decision to leave our evil ways for God.

---

[17] Revelation 13:8, John 1:29-36
[18] 1John 2:2

All we like sheep have gone astray; we have turned every one to his own way; and the LORD [God] has laid on him [Jesus] the iniquity [rebellion, waywardness] of us all. (Isaiah 53:6)

How do you receive this gift? You have to bow your knee in full submission to the risen King, Jesus, acknowledging him as Lord.[19] This kind of commitment is not cheap; nor can it be forced on you by anybody. It's got to be a genuine act, from the heart. When you allow Jesus—the highest King—into your life, he comes in as the KING. You submit to him, and the GREAT BENEFIT of having him in your life, is that he *saves* you. The mercy of the cross is applied to your life, *forever.*

I urge you to chose God, your Creator, the only one who can give you eternal life and so many *wonderful, indescribable* things in this life. Though the path will not be easy, God will give you supernatural peace, joy, many gifts, knowledge of him, wisdom, mental and physical healing, and so much more. But the entrance into this life is like a narrow gate. You've gotta make the full-on TRUST choice, to let go of your life and hand it over to God, it's rightful owner.

Bow to the Messiah-King, Jesus, and submit full allegiance to Him. Then he will save you, as you call out to him. He will forgive you of *ALL* past sins—He alone can do that—if you wholeheartedly leave them for Him. He will cleanse your conscience and give you a new heart.

Scripture says, "Everyone who believes in him will not be put to shame." For there is no distinction between Jew and Greek

---

[19] "Lord" means "Authority"

[or any others]; for the same Lord is Lord of all, bestowing his riches on all who call on him. For "everyone who calls on the name of the Lord will be saved." (Romans 10:11-13)

Don't wait. The act that Jesus commands you to do, along with calling on Him to save you, is baptism, that is, immersion[20] in water.

After Jesus rose from the dead, he appeared to hundreds of his disciples[21] for a period of forty days, and he told them these things:

All authority in heaven and on earth has been given to me. Go therefore and make disciples of all nations, baptizing them [i.e., immersing them in water]. [Do this] in the name[22] of the Father and of the Son and of the Holy Spirit, teaching them to observe all that I have commanded you. And behold, I am with you every day, to the end of the age. (Matthew 28:18-20)

And he said to them, "Go into all the world and proclaim the gospel[23] to the whole creation. Whoever believes and is baptized ["immersed"] will be saved, but whoever does not believe will be condemned. And these signs will accompany those who believe: in my name they will cast out demons[24]; they will speak in new tongues[25]; they will pick up serpents with their hands; and if they drink any deadly poison, it will not hurt them; they will lay their hands on the sick, and they

---

[20] "Baptism" literally means "immersion"

[21] "Disciple" means "Student" or "Apprentice"

[22] In other words, "in the authority of"

[23] "Gospel" means, "Good News"

[24] "Demons" means evil spirits

[25] Languages (a supernatural gift for all who believe)

will recover." So then the Lord Jesus, after he had spoken to them, was taken up into heaven and sat down at the right hand of God. And they went out and preached everywhere, while the Lord worked with them and confirmed the message by accompanying [supernatural] signs. (Mark 16:15-20)

The last work Jesus did while on Earth was to send his apprentices out into all the world, with the mission of telling "the Gospel," the good news about Jesus—who He is, what he did for the world on the cross, and what he will do for them personally if they accept him as King. He also gave them a promise: he would be with them as they went and he would back the message up with miraculous signs. This promise is true today. As one of Jesus' apprentices, I am telling you God's message. He wants you to be close to him, so much so he sacrificed his Son Jesus, so you can live and know him. He CAN forgive your sins—no matter how great—because Jesus took your death penalty already. That's how much love he has for you. He will accept you and save you from death and judgment, if you let go of your sins to follow Jesus.

If you are sick or have pain right now, place your hand on the problem area and hear these words, which I speak for you: "Jesus, I know you love this person, and you want them to be yours. In the authority of Jesus, I command the pain, sickness, and disability of the person's body: be healed. Any spirit of affliction attacking this person against their will, go now!"

Lesson 2

How Jesus Deals With the *ROOTS*

It's wonderful, GOOD NEWS that God deals with the roots of our problems. What we would overlook and not even address, he sees clearly and decided to provide a Solution for. Consider this conversation King Jesus had with a political and religious leader in Israel:

Now there was a man of the Pharisees[26] named Nicodemus, a ruler of the Jews.[27] This man came to Jesus by night[28] and said to him, "Rabbi, we know that you are a teacher come from God, for no one can do these signs that you do unless God is with him." Jesus answered him, "Truly, truly, I say to you, unless one is born again he cannot see the kingdom[29] of God. (John 3:1-3)

---

[26] A religious group of that day; they were very devout, but most of them were so blind that they missed the promised Messiah, and gave him over to be crucified. Their religion wasn't enough; they needed a Savior

[27] The Book of John was written partly to Gentiles (non-Jews), so often the term "the Jews" is used, since Jesus only worked in Israel while on Earth. "Jews," in the Book of John, sometimes refers to people from the province of Judea, which included Jerusalem (see John 11:7-8). Sometimes it refers to all "Hebrews," as the term is used today, those descended from Abraham, Isaac, and Jacob (see John 4:22). In this sense, Jesus is a Jew, as is John, the writer of this book, though they were not from Judea but Galilee, another province in Israel

[28] He came by night because of fear. The whole atmosphere of Judea at that time was tense because of threats from the political & religious leaders. They envied, and hated Jesus, because of his teaching and miracles, and used fear to keep people from following him (see John 9:22, 12:42)

[29] The "kingdom of God" means God's domain, his territory or country, his reign, and his government

With this statement, Jesus brought out a truth that is invaluable: without a new birth, the human race can never even see God's kingdom.

Nicodemus said to him, "How can a man be born when he is old? Can he enter a second time into his mother's womb and be born?" (John 3:4)

Man cannot know what he is without revelation from God. At man's creation, God formed man's body of the dust of the Earth, but he had no life until God breathed into his nostrils. Then man became a living being.[30] What entered man's body was the human spirit and soul. Man was now living in his earthly body, with a mind and emotions. The term "soul" in the Bible often refers to a person's mind and emotions.[31]

The first woman was made after man had been created. She was actually taken out of the man.[32] Both of them, then, had a spirit, a soul, and a body. These three elements make up what a human being is.[33]

It is so important to understand this next valuable truth:

God created man in his own image, in the image of God he created him; male and female he created him. (Genesis 1:27)

When God created man, he did so very, *very* differently than the way he created animals. He used his creativity to make a huge

---

[30] Genesis 2:7
[31] "Soul" also sometimes also means, "being," and sometimes, "self-centered will," depending on context
[32] Genesis 2:18-25
[33] 1Thessalonians 5:23

diversity of living beings, but when it came to mankind, he used his own image to create them.

Notice also that it's the combination of a male and female which is the complete image of God. God encompasses both.

Now let's come to why Jesus taught that mankind must be reborn. In the Garden, after creating man and woman, God considered his creation "very good."[34] By looking at the world today, we see that it is not "very good" anymore, and we understand that there was a fall.

The Lord God commanded the man, saying, "You may surely eat of every tree of the garden, but of the tree of the knowledge of good and evil you shall not eat, for in the day that you eat of it you shall surely die. (Genesis 2:16-17)

What part of man and woman died on the day they ate the forbidden fruit? It was not their mind—they kept on thinking and living once expelled from the Garden. Their bodies kept on living as well for a while. It was their spirit, the essence of who they were, the connection they had to God and to the spiritual realms.

It's hard for us to understand death outside of the physical realm. What does it mean that their spirit died? At least part of the answer is that it was cut off from God. It lost connection to God, the source of its life and light. Afterward, as Adam and Eve reproduced, all their children were born with the same lack of connection to God. All humanity was born dead spiritually, but Jesus, though born as a man, was born alive.[35]

---

[34] Genesis 1:31

[35] Through what's been called, "the immaculate conception." See Luke 1:31-37

When Jesus was sent to solve the problems of mankind, his job started at the roots—saving man's spirit.

Jesus answered, "Truly, truly, I say to you, unless one is born of water and the Spirit, he cannot enter the kingdom of God. That which is born of the flesh is flesh, and that which is born of the Spirit is spirit. Do not marvel that I said to you, 'You must be born again.' The wind blows where it wishes, and you hear its sound, but you do not know where it comes from or where it goes. So it is with everyone who is born of the Spirit. (John 3:5-8)

Being "born of flesh" refers to our physical body. To be "born again" means to be "born of the Spirit." It refers to our spirit. This Spirit is the "Spirit of God," introduced in the very beginning of Genesis. He's part of God.

Jesus came to bring *life* to the earth, a kind of life that was lost by mankind. At one point, Jesus was speaking with a crowd of people:

Jesus then said to them, "Truly, truly, I say to you, it was not Moses who gave you the bread from heaven,[36] but my Father gives you the true bread from heaven. For the bread of God is he who comes down from heaven and gives life to the world." They said to him, "Sir, give us this bread always." Jesus said to them, "I am the bread of life; whoever comes to me will not

[36] God used Moses to lead his People—the descendants of Abraham, Isaac, and Jacob—out of slavery in Egypt. He led them into the desert, on the way to a land he'd promised to give them. In the desert, he provided for them supernaturally, including their food ("Manna"). However, that food was only a shadow of the true bread from Heaven, Jesus

hunger, and whoever believes in me will never thirst. But I said to you that you have seen me and yet do not believe. All that the Father gives me will come to me, and whoever comes to me I will never cast out. For I have come down from heaven, not to do my own will but the will of him who sent me. And this is the will of him who sent me, that I should lose nothing of all that he has given me, but raise it up on the last day. For this is the will of my Father, that everyone who looks on the Son and believes in him should have eternal life, and I will raise him up on the last day."

So the Jews grumbled about him, because he said, "I am the bread that came down from heaven." They said, "Is not this Jesus, the son of Joseph, whose father and mother we know? How does he now say, 'I have come down from heaven'?" Jesus answered them, "Do not grumble among yourselves. No one can come to me unless the Father who sent me draws him. And I will raise him up on the last day. It is written in the Prophets, 'And they will all be taught by God.' Everyone who has heard and learned from the Father comes to me—not that anyone has seen the Father except he who is from God; he has seen the Father.

Truly, truly, I say to you, whoever believes has eternal life. I am the bread of life. Your fathers ate the manna in the wilderness, and they died. This is the bread that comes down from heaven, so that one may eat of it and not die. I am the living bread that came down from heaven. If anyone eats of this bread, he will live forever. And the bread that I will give for the life of the world is my flesh. The Judeans then disputed among themselves, saying, "How can this man give us his flesh to eat?" So Jesus said to them, "Truly, truly, I say to you, unless you eat the flesh of the Son of Man and drink his blood, you have no life in you. Whoever feeds on my flesh and drinks my blood has eternal life, and I will raise him up on the last day. For my flesh is true food, and my blood is true drink. Whoever feeds on my flesh and drinks my blood abides in me, and I in him. As the living Father sent me, and I live because of the Father, so whoever feeds on me, he also will live because of me. (John 6:32-57)

Do you want to live? If this is making sense to you at all, God is already inviting you to his Son Jesus, so you can receive life. You will receive spiritual life; you will be born again. And this life goes on forever.

Lesson 3

Immersion in Water

When Jesus rose from the dead, he interacted with his apprentices of that time for forty days. At the end of this time, the King gave them a commission, which included these words.

He said to them, "Go into all the world and proclaim the gospel to the whole creation. Whoever believes and is baptized will be saved, but whoever does not believe will be condemned.... (Mark 16:15-16)

Shortly after King Jesus commissioned his apprentices and ascended, Peter spoke to a large crowd in Jerusalem, where Jesus had just been crucified. The crowd was astonished to realize that they'd missed God's chosen Messiah for them, and let him be crucified!!! They were cut to the heart as they believed the truth they heard. Peter shouted out at the end of his message:

"...Let all the house of Israel therefore know for certain that God has made him both Lord and Christ [or, "Messiah"], this Jesus whom you crucified." Now when they heard this they were cut to the heart, and said to Peter and the rest of the apostles, "Brothers, what shall we do?" And Peter said to them, "Repent and be baptized every one of you in the name of Jesus Christ for the forgiveness of your sins, and you will receive the gift of the Holy Spirit. The promise is for you and your children and for all who are far off—for all whom the Lord our God will call." With many other words he warned

them; and he pleaded with them, "Save yourselves from this corrupt generation." Those who accepted his message were baptized, and about three thousand were added to their number that day. (Acts 2:36-41)

They'd made a big, BIG mistake. But God is merciful. He provided a Solution to their dilemma—Jesus' death, the very thing they were partially guilty of! God is a merciful forgiver of sins. He was willing to forgive and save them. The fact that they just helped crucify His Son did not stop him, because He IS love, and he is able to forgive.

In verse 38, above, Peter told them how to respond to the Good News: repent and be immersed in water. To "repent" means to *change*. It's a change of heart that will result in a change of life. These people had been against their Messiah, Jesus, but it was now time for them to change, to make him their Lord, to call on him to save them. Their WHOLE LIFE would be affected totally by this change. The same is true for you, friend.

In Jesus commission, another thing he said was,

"Thus it is written, that the Christ should suffer and on the third day rise from the dead, and that repentance and forgiveness of sins should be proclaimed in his name to all nations, beginning from Jerusalem" (Luke 24:46-47)

Notice that changing the way you think ("repentance") comes *before* forgiveness of sins. If a person doesn't truly bow to the Authority, Jesus, from the heart, in light of the Message, that person *cannot* obtain forgiveness. Forgiveness is in the authority of the Messiah Jesus, and in His authority alone, as God sent *HIM* as the savior. You try to get God's forgiveness any other way, and He won't give it to you.

This Jesus is the stone that was rejected by you[37], the builders, which has become the cornerstone. And there is salvation in no one else, for there is no other name[38] under heaven given among men by which we must be saved. (Acts 4:11-12)

Maybe you've even heard of Jesus and even agreed that he rose from the dead, but haven't personally submitted to him as Lord, directly. Now is the time.

On one occasion, Jesus used a man named Ananias to heal someone who had been struck blind. The healed man recounted what happened to him in the Book of Acts, in Scripture:

"A man named Ananias came to see me. He was a devout observer of the law[39] and highly respected by all the Jews living there. He stood beside me and said, 'Brother Saul, receive your sight!' And at that very moment I was able to see him. "Then he said: 'The God of our ancestors has chosen you to know his will and to see the Righteous One and to hear words from his mouth. You will be his witness to all people of what you have seen and heard. And now what are you waiting

---

[37] Jesus' apprentice, Peter, was speaking to his fellow Jews in Jerusalem in this verse, who had shortly before rejected their Messiah, having not recognized his humble form

[38] Or, "authority"

[39] The Law of Moses, given to the Jews before the prophesied Messiah came. Ananias was also a follower of the Messiah-King Jesus, who the Law pointed to

for? *Get up, be baptized and wash your sins away, calling on his name.'* (Acts 22:12-16)

Your next and immediate step is to be baptized—immersed in water.

Find an apprentice of Jesus, a sincere follower of Jesus, and ask them to immerse you in water. You can use any body of water—a river, lake, swimming pool, a bathtub, a water tank, etc. You don't need a religious leader to do it, just a follower of Jesus.[40] What makes it effective is your sincere faith in Jesus and change of heart toward God.

Recognize that this is a commitment you are making before God, pledging yourself to Him.[41] You're not being immersed into *any* human organization or "church," but into "the name (or "authority") of Jesus."[42] You connect with God and His Kingdom as you're immersed. You are being "immersed into Jesus' death" so that you join with him also in His resurrection life.[43] This is why it is soooo powerful.

One woman I know of made Jesus her Lord in a dangerously oppressive country. She could not find anyone to baptize her, including the Christians she new, so she had to immerse herself in the Name of the Lord Jesus.[44] Though typically another follower of

---

[40] Because of man-made, religious tradition, the person may hesitate, try to postpone it or to get a religious leader to do it—if so you may need to find someone else. The Bible shows new converts always being immersed immediately after choosing Jesus, according to Jesus' command, and any believer can do it

[41] 1Peter 3:21

[42] Acts 2:38, 10:48

[43] Romans 6:3-4, Colossians 2:12

[44] Her story is in her book, "I Dared to Call Him Father."

Jesus is to immerse a new disciple, this woman did the right thing in obedience to her new King. It changed her life.

Again, it's immersion "in the name of Jesus," meaning it's spiritual and covered by His authority. So it will have a powerful effect on your life. As you do it you are to commit yourself to God, and call on Him to save you. It's the first step of your total change toward God and faith in Jesus. The physical act gives a picture of what's happening, that your sins, which have been forgiven, are being washed away, and your old nature of rebellion against God is being buried with Jesus. You are also rising to walk in new, resurrection life.

If you feel any invisible resistance in this process, it's demonic. Command it to go; don't let it stand between you and your immersion. The authority and power of the risen King Jesus will be with you to move every evil force out of your way, and they *will* lose their power. Press forward, eyes on Jesus. Ask him for help if you need it, and press on.

For a new believer, immersion is totally urgent.[45] Be immersed in water right away, without delay.

After you've been immersed in water, you can download the full, PDF version of this book, "Jesus the King," for free, here:

www.actschristianity.com

It includes a section called, "First Steps," to help you grow on Jesus' narrow path to Life. The very next step you'll learn about learn about is another gift from God, promised to all who repent and are immersed in water: "immersion in the Holy Spirit."

---

[45] Acts 16:33, Acts 2216, Acts 10:48, Acts 8:35-38

www.ingramcontent.com/pod-product-compliance
Lightning Source LLC
Chambersburg PA
CBHW060607030426
42337CB00019B/3641